Whitewater Rafting

by Michèle Dufresne

Pioneer Valley Educational Press, Inc.

Whitewater rafting is fun.

Whitewater rafting
can be **dangerous**.
Put on your **life jacket**!

Here is a whitewater raft.
A whitewater raft is an
inflatable boat.

Here are **paddles** for the raft.

The water can be fun.
The water can be dangerous, too.

Look out for rocks
in the water.
Look out for **waterfalls**.

Rocks in the water
and waterfalls
can make rafting dangerous.

Whitewater Rafting

dangerous

inflatable boat

life jacket

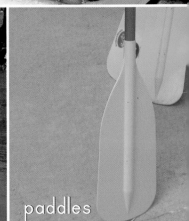

paddles

waterfall

16